THROUGH THE LOOKING-GLASS

'You can be the White Queen's pawn,' the Red Queen tells Alice. 'A pawn goes two squares in its first move. So you'll go *very* quickly through the Third Square – by railway, probably. Then in the Fourth Square you'll meet Tweedledum and Tweedledee. The Fifth Square is mostly water, and the Sixth belongs to Humpty Dumpty. The Seventh Square is all forest – one of the Knights will show you the way.'

And in the Eighth Square Alice will become a Queen. But what a strange game of chess it is! In the looking-glass world all the chess pieces argue with you, and you have to run very fast just to stay in the same place. Here, time runs backwards and the White Queen can remember what happened the week after next.

And whose dream is it, anyway? Is it Alice's dream, or is she just a part of the Red King's dream? And if so, what will happen if he wakes up?

OXFORD BOOKWORMS LIBRARY
Classics

Through the Looking-Glass

Stage 3 (1000 headwords)

Series Editor: Jennifer Bassett
Founder Editor: Tricia Hedge
Activities Editors: Jennifer Bassett and Christine Lindop

LEWIS CARROLL

Through the Looking-Glass

And What Alice Found There

Retold by
Jennifer Bassett

With original illustrations by
John Tenniel

OXFORD UNIVERSITY PRESS

2000

Oxford University Press
Great Clarendon Street, Oxford OX2 6DP

Oxford New York
Athens Auckland Bangkok Bogotá Buenos Aires Calcutta Cape Town
Chennai Dar es Salaam Delhi Florence Hong Kong Istanbul Karachi
Kuala Lumpur Madrid Melbourne Mexico City Mumbai Nairobi
Paris São Paulo Shanghai Singapore Taipei Tokyo Toronto Warsaw
and associated companies in
Berlin Ibadan

OXFORD and OXFORD ENGLISH
are trade marks of Oxford University Press

ISBN 0 19 423019 8

This simplified edition © Oxford University Press 2000

Second impression 2000

First published in Oxford Bookworms 1995
This second edition published in the Oxford Bookworms Library 2000

Printed in Spain by Unigraf s.l.

CONTENTS

STORY INTRODUCTION   i

THE GAME OF CHESS   viii

 1 Looking-glass house   1

 2 The garden of live flowers   6

 3 Looking-glass animals   13

 4 Tweedledum and Tweedledee   17

 5 The White Queen   22

 6 Humpty Dumpty   29

 7 The Lion and the Unicorn   34

 8 The White Knight   42

 9 Queen Alice   49

10 Shaking   55

11 Waking   56

12 Who dreamed it?   56

    GLOSSARY   58

    ACTIVITIES: Before Reading   60

    ACTIVITIES: While Reading   61

    ACTIVITIES: After Reading   64

    ABOUT THE AUTHOR   68

    ABOUT BOOKWORMS   69

THE GAME OF CHESS

Chess is a game for two people, played on a chess-board marked with sixty-four black and white squares. The thirty-two chess pieces – also called chessmen – are black (or red) and white, and are called kings, queens, bishops, knights, castles (or rooks), and pawns. The pawn is the smallest and least important piece.

If a pawn reaches the eighth square on the opposite side of the board, it can be exchanged for a queen. This is what happens to Alice in the story.

CHARACTERS IN THE STORY

CHESSMEN

The White Queen	The Red Queen
The White King	The Red King
The White Knight	The Red Knight

OTHER CHARACTERS

Talking flowers, *Tiger-lily, Rose, Daisy*
Tweedledum and Tweedledee
Humpty Dumpty
The Lion and the Unicorn
Haigha and Hatta, *the White King's messengers*

1
Looking-glass house

One thing was certain, it was the *black* kitten that began it all. The white kitten had been unable to do anything for the last quarter of an hour, because the old cat was washing its face, very slowly and very carefully.

But the black kitten was free to do what it wanted. And so, while Alice was sitting in a corner of the great armchair, half talking to herself and half asleep, the kitten was playing a grand game with a ball of wool. Soon the wool was lying in a terrible tangle all over the carpet, with the kitten running after its own tail in the middle.

'Oh, you bad little thing!' cried Alice, when she saw the wool. She picked up the kitten and climbed back into the armchair. 'You really mustn't play with the wool, you know. It will take me so long to roll the ball up again. Why don't you play chess instead, Kitty? When I was playing a while ago, you were watching me so carefully. In fact, you look just like the Red Queen yourself.'

And Alice picked up the Red Queen from the chessmen on the table, and held it up to show the kitten. But the kitten tried to escape, and, to punish it, Alice lifted it up to the looking-glass above the fireplace. 'If you're not good, Kitty,' she said, 'I'll put you through into looking-glass house. How would you like *that*?

'I do wonder,' Alice went on, 'if everything in that room is the same as in our room. The things that I can see *look* the same – except the books, because the words go the wrong way. But perhaps the rest of the house is really different and full of interesting things. Oh, I wish we could get through, Kitty! Let's pretend we can. Let's pretend the glass has gone soft and . . . Why, I do believe it has! It's turning into a kind of cloud . . .'

Alice did not know how it happened, but while she was speaking, she found herself climbing up to the looking-glass. And the glass was beginning to disappear, just like a bright silvery cloud.

In another moment Alice was through the glass and had jumped down into the looking-glass room. At once she began looking around and noticed that several things were very different from the old room. The pictures on the wall all seemed to be alive, and the clock above the fireplace had the face of a little old man, who smiled at her.

'This room isn't as tidy as the other one,' Alice thought to herself, as she noticed several chessmen on the floor by the fireplace. But the next moment, with a little 'Oh!' of surprise, she was down on the floor herself, watching them.

The chessmen were walking around, arm in arm!

'Here are the Red King and the Red Queen,' Alice said, in a whisper, in order not to frighten them. 'And there are two Castles walking together. And two of the Pawns, and a white Bishop reading a newspaper . . . I don't think they can hear me or see me,' she went on. 'I wonder—'

Then something on the table behind her made a noise. Alice turned to look and saw that one of the White Pawns had fallen over and begun to cry. She watched it with interest.

'It is the voice of my child!' cried the White Queen by the fireplace. 'My dear Lily! My sweet child!' and she began to

'Here are the Red King and the Red Queen,' Alice said.

3

climb wildly up the table leg.

Poor little Lily was now screaming loudly. Alice wanted to be helpful, so she picked up the Queen and put her on the table next to her noisy little daughter.

The Queen sat very still, with her mouth open, for almost a minute. Then she called down to the White King, who was still on the floor by the fireplace. 'Be careful of the storm!'

'What storm?' said the King, looking round worriedly.

'There's a terrible wind – it blew me up here in a second. You come up the usual way, and be careful!'

Alice watched as the White King slowly began to climb the table leg. Then she said, 'It will take you hours to get up. Why don't I help you?' Gently, she picked him up and moved him slowly upwards. The King was very surprised indeed. His eyes and his mouth got larger and larger, and rounder and

The King was very surprised indeed.

rounder. Alice nearly dropped him because she was laughing so much.

When she put him down on the table, he immediately fell flat on his back and lay still. But after a while he sat up, and spoke to the Queen in a frightened whisper.

'I tell you, my dear, I turned cold to the very ends of my hair! I shall never, *never* forget that moment.'

'You will,' the Queen said, 'if you don't write it down.'

Alice watched with interest as the King took out a very large notebook and began writing. Then she saw a book lying on the table near her, and began to turn the pages.

'It's all in some language that I don't know,' she said to herself. It was like this.

ЈАВВЕRWOCKY

'Twas brillig, and the slithy toves
Did gyre and gimble in the wabe;
All mimsy were the borogoves,
And the mome raths outgrabe.

Puzzled, she looked at it for some time, then suddenly understood. 'Of course, it's a looking-glass book! If I hold it up to the glass, the words will go the right way again.'

This was the poem that Alice read.

JABBERWOCKY

'Twas brillig, and the slithy toves
Did gyre and gimble in the wabe;
All mimsy were the borogoves,
And the mome raths outgrabe.

'It seems very pretty,' Alice said, 'but a little hard to

understand.' (Actually, she didn't understand a word of it, but didn't like to say so.) 'It seems to fill my head with ideas – but I don't know what they are!'

Then she suddenly jumped up, as another idea came to her. 'If I don't hurry, I shall have to go back through the looking-glass before I've seen the rest of the house, and the garden. I'll look at the garden first, I think.'

In a moment she was out of the room and running down the stairs. But it wasn't really running, because she was moving gently through the air and her feet weren't touching the stairs at all. At the bottom she managed to catch hold of the door-post, and after that she was pleased to find herself walking again in a natural way.

2

The garden of live flowers

There was a small hill not far away and Alice decided to walk to it. 'I shall be able to see the garden better from the top of the hill,' she said.

She tried very hard to reach the hill, but it seemed impossible to get to it. She went first this way, then that way, but every time she turned a corner, she found herself back at the house.

'I'm *not* going in again yet,' she told the house crossly. 'I'll have to go back through the looking-glass into the old room and that's the end of all my adventures then!'

She tried once more, and this time passed a large flowerbed, with a tree growing in the middle.

'Oh Tiger-lily,' Alice said to one of the flowers, 'I wish you could talk!'

'We *can* talk,' said the Tiger-lily, 'if there is anybody interesting enough to talk to.'

For a minute Alice was too surprised to speak. Then she said,

'We can talk,' said the Tiger-lily,
'if there is anybody interesting enough to talk to.'

almost in a whisper, 'And can *all* the flowers talk?'

'As well as *you* can,' said the Tiger-lily. 'And a lot louder.'

'It isn't polite for us to begin, you know,' said the Rose, 'and I was really wondering when you would speak.'

'But why can you all talk?' Alice said, puzzled. 'I've been in many gardens before, and none of the flowers could talk.'

'Put your hand down and feel the ground,' said the Tiger-lily. 'Then you'll know why.'

Alice did so. 'It's very hard,' she said, 'but how does that explain it?'

'In most gardens,' the Tiger-lily said, 'they make the flower-beds too soft – so the flowers are always asleep.'

This sounded a very good reason to Alice. 'I never thought of that before!' she said.

'Do you ever think *at all*?' asked the Rose, unkindly.

'I never saw anybody with a more stupid face,' said a Daisy suddenly. It was the first time it had spoken, and Alice jumped in surprise.

'Oh, be quiet!' cried the Tiger-lily. 'What do you Daisies know about the world?'

'Are there any other people in the garden?' Alice asked.

'There's one other flower that can move around like you,' said the Rose. 'She's the same strange shape as you, but she's redder, with more leaves than you have.'

'She's coming now!' cried another Daisy. 'I can hear her feet – bang, bang, bang, on the ground.'

Alice looked round quickly, and saw that it was the Red Queen. 'She's grown a lot,' Alice thought. When she had seen her by the fireplace, the Queen had been only eight centimetres high. Now she was taller than Alice herself!

'I think I'll go and meet her,' Alice said.

'You can't possibly do that,' said the Rose. 'You must walk the other way if you want to meet her.'

This sounded nonsense to Alice, so she began to walk towards the Red Queen. To her surprise, she found herself a minute later walking in through the front door of the house. She turned round crossly, and saw the Queen again, on the other side of the garden. This time she tried walking the other way, *away* from the Queen.

It succeeded beautifully. A minute later she was standing opposite the Red Queen, and very near the hill that she had wanted to get to.

'Where do you come from?' said the Red Queen. 'Where are you going? And why are you here at all? Look up, speak nicely, keep your hands still. And curtsy while you're thinking what to say. It saves time.'

Alice tried to obey all these orders, feeling just a little frightened of the Queen.

'I only wanted to look at the garden, your Majesty, from the top of that hill,' she began.

'Hill!' cried the Queen. 'Some people would call that a valley.'

'But a hill *can't* be a valley,' said Alice. 'That would be nonsense.'

The Red Queen shook her head. 'You can call it nonsense if you like. Some people would say it was sensible!'

'It's just like a large chess-board!' Alice said.

Alice curtsied again, and decided it would be safer not to argue any more. Together, they walked on in silence up the hill. At the top Alice could see right across the country – and a very strange country it was. There were lots of little brooks running across from side to side, and there were long lines of hedges, going the other way. It was a country of squares.

'It's just like a large chess-board!' Alice said at last. 'Oh, and I can see some chessmen down there!' Her heart began to beat fast with excitement. 'It's a great game of chess, as big as the world itself – if this *is* the world at all. Oh, what fun! I wish I could be in it, even as a Pawn. Although I would love to be a Queen, of course.'

She looked a little worriedly at the real Queen as she said this. But the Red Queen smiled kindly, and said, 'You can be the White Queen's Pawn, if you like. Lily is too young to play. You're in the Second Square now, and when you get to the

Eighth Square, you'll be a Queen—'

Just at that moment, they began to run. Alice never did understand how it happened, but she had no time to think about it because they were running so fast.

'Faster! Faster!' cried the Queen, pulling Alice's hand. They ran like the wind, but the strange thing was that they never seemed to pass anything. The trees and other things round them never changed their places at all.

Alice was very puzzled by this, but still the Queen cried, 'Faster! Faster!' Now they were almost flying over the ground. Alice had never run so fast in her life.

When at last they stopped, she had to sit down because her legs were shaking. Then she looked around in surprise.

'But we've been under this same tree all the time! We're still in the same place!'

'Of course we are,' said the Queen. 'Why shouldn't we be?'

'Faster! Faster!' cried the Queen.

'Well, in our country,' said Alice, 'if you run very fast for a long time, you usually arrive at a different place.'

'What a slow kind of country!' said the Queen. 'Here, you see, you have to run very fast, just to keep in the same place. If you want to go somewhere different, you must run twice as fast. Now,' she went on, 'I shall tell you what to do. While I'm speaking, I shall take five steps, and at the fifth step, I shall go.'

She took two steps away from the tree and turned round. 'A pawn goes two squares in its first move. So you'll go *very* quickly through the Third Square – by railway, probably. Then you'll be in the Fourth Square, which belongs to Tweedledum and Tweedledee. The Fifth Square is mostly water, and the Sixth belongs to Humpty Dumpty. But why haven't you said anything?'

'I didn't know I had to say anything,' said Alice.

'It's polite,' said the Queen, 'to say thank you for all this information. But never mind. Let's pretend you said it. The Seventh Square is all forest – one of the Knights will show you the way – and in the Eighth Square we shall be Queens together, and it's all parties and fun!'

Alice got up and curtsied, and sat down again.

The Queen took another two steps and turned round again. 'Speak in French when you can't think of the English word – and always remember who you are!'

She took another step, and was gone. Alice did not know if she had disappeared into the air, or run into the wood. But she had certainly gone, and Alice began to remember that she was a Pawn, and that it would soon be time to move.

3
Looking-glass animals

Alice stood at the top of the hill and looked down. 'Which way should I go?' she wondered. On one side she could see, a long way away, some kind of large animals walking around. She wasn't sure that she liked the look of them, so she decided to go the other way. She ran down the hill and jumped over the first of the six little brooks.

* * * * *
* * * *
* * * * *

'Tickets, please!' said the Ticket Inspector, putting his head in at the window. In a moment everybody was holding out a ticket; the tickets were almost as big as the people, and seemed to fill the train.

'Show your ticket, child!' the Inspector went on, looking angrily at Alice. And then several voices said all together, 'Don't keep him waiting, child! His time costs a thousand pounds a minute!'

'I'm afraid I haven't got a ticket,' Alice said in a frightened voice. 'There wasn't a ticket-office where I came from.'

'Why didn't you buy one from the engine-driver?' said the Inspector. And again the voices said, 'The engine-driver's time costs a thousand pounds a minute!'

The Inspector looked at Alice first through his glasses, then over the top of them. Then he said, 'You're travelling the wrong way,' and shut up the window and went away.

'She ought to know which way she's going,' said the gentleman sitting opposite Alice (he was dressed in white paper), 'but perhaps she doesn't know her own name.'

A Goat, that was sitting next to the gentleman in white, said loudly, 'She ought to know her way to the ticket-office, but perhaps she can't read or write.'

There was a Beetle next to the Goat, and he had something to say about Alice as well. Then other voices spoke, but Alice could not see who they were. One voice sounded like a horse, she thought. And then a very small voice, right next to her ear, said, 'You could make a poem out of that – something about "a horse, of course".'

The gentleman in white paper spoke again. 'Don't worry,

A Goat was sitting next to the gentleman in white.

my dear,' he whispered. 'Just buy a return ticket every time the train stops.'

'No, I won't!' Alice said crossly. 'I don't belong to this railway journey at all. I was in a wood just now, and I wish I could get back there.'

Then she heard the little voice again. She looked round, but could see nothing. 'I know you are a friend,' the voice said in her ear, 'a dear friend. And you won't hurt me, although I am an insect.'

'What kind of insect?' Alice asked, a little worried. But just then there came a long scream from the engine, and everybody jumped up. The Horse put his head out of the window, then pulled it back in and said calmly, 'It's only a brook that we have to jump across.'

Alice did not like the idea of trains jumping brooks. 'But we'll get into the Fourth Square, I suppose,' she said to herself. In another moment she felt the train go straight up into the air. Frightened, she caught at the thing nearest to her hand, which happened to be the Goat's beard.

*　*　*　*　*

*　*　*　*

*　*　*　*　*

But the beard seemed to disappear as she touched it, and she found herself sitting quietly under a tree. There was an Insect sitting near her, on a low branch of the tree.

It was a very large insect indeed – almost as big as a chicken, Alice thought.

'So you don't like all insects?' the Insect said, quietly continuing their conversation.

15

'I like them when they can talk,' Alice said. 'None of them ever talk, where *I* come from. But everything here is so different. I probably don't even know the names of the insects here.'

'Can you remember your own name?' asked the Insect.

'Of course,' said Alice. 'Nobody forgets their own name.'

'Don't they?' said the Insect. 'There's a wood down there, for example, where things have no names.'

Alice looked round, and saw a dark wood on the other side of an open field. When she looked back, the Insect had flown away. She got up and began to walk across the field. 'This must be the way to the Eighth Square,' she thought, 'but I hope I don't lose my name in this wood.'

She soon reached the wood and was pleased to get out of the hot sun and into the shadows under the trees. 'How nice and cool it is in here, under the . . . under the . . . under the *what?*' she said, surprised that she could not think of the word. She put her hand on a tree. 'What *does* it call itself? I do believe it's got no name!'

She stood for a moment, thinking. 'And now, who am I? I *will* remember, if I can.' She tried and tried, but she just could not remember her name. It began with an 'L', she thought, but she wasn't really sure.

So she hurried on through the wood, hoping to get to the other side quickly, and after a while she came out into another open field. She stopped, and thought hard. 'Why, it's Alice, of course!' she said. 'My name's Alice – I won't forget it again. And now, which way should I go?'

It was not a difficult question to answer. There was only

one road, and a large signpost, which said:

To Tweedledum's House

To the House of Tweedledee

'I'll just call in and say hello,' Alice said, 'and ask them the way to the Eighth Square. I *would* like to get there before it gets dark.' So she walked on, talking to herself as she went. After a long time the road came into another wood and suddenly turned a corner, and there in front of her Alice saw two fat little men standing under a tree.

4

Tweedledum and Tweedledee

Alice knew immediately which one was which, because each had his name on his shirt. They were standing very still, with their arms round each other, and Alice forgot that they were alive. 'They look just like schoolboys,' she said aloud. Then one of them spoke, and Alice jumped in surprise.

'You've begun wrong!' cried the one called Tweedledum. 'The first thing in a visit is to say "How do you do?" and shake hands.' And here the brothers held out the two hands that were free, to shake hands with her.

Alice did not know which hand to shake first, so she took hold of both hands at once. The next moment they were all three dancing round in a circle. This seemed very natural at the time, and Alice was not even surprised to hear music playing.

'They look *just like schoolboys,*' Alice said aloud.

The two brothers were fat, and soon got tired. 'Four times round is enough for one dance,' Tweedledee said, and they stopped as suddenly as they had begun. Then they stood looking at Alice in silence.

Alice did not know what to say. How do you begin a conversation with people that you have just been dancing with? she wondered.

'I hope you're not too tired?' she said at last.

'Not at all. And thank you *very* much for asking,' said Tweedledum.

'*Very* kind of you,' added Tweedledee. 'Do you like poems?'

'Ye–es ... well, *some* poems,' Alice said carefully. 'Would

18

you tell me which road to take out of the wood?'

'What shall I repeat to her?' Tweedledee said to Tweedledum, not noticing Alice's question.

'*The Walrus and the Carpenter* is the longest,' Tweedledum replied, putting a friendly arm round his brother.

'If it's *very* long,' Alice said politely, 'would you tell me first which road—'

Tweedledee smiled gently and began his poem. It was a very long poem indeed – all about a Walrus and a Carpenter, who went for a walk along a beach and invited lots of young Oysters to go with them. The Oysters accepted happily.

'Perhaps that wasn't very sensible of them,' Alice said.

Tweedledee only smiled, and continued:

> *The Walrus and the Carpenter*
> *Walked on a mile or so,*
> *And then they rested on a rock*
> *Conveniently low;*
> *And all the little Oysters stood*
> *And waited in a row.*
> *'The time has come,' the Walrus said,*
> *'To talk of many things:*
> *Of shoes—and ships—and sealing-wax—*
> *Of cabbages—and kings—*
> *And why the sea is boiling hot—*
> *And whether pigs have wings.'*

Alice waited with interest to hear about this conversation, but it never happened, because the Walrus and the Carpenter went on to eat all the Oysters instead.

And all the little Oysters stood
And waited in a row.

At the end Alice said, 'I like the Walrus best, because he said he felt sorry for the poor Oysters.'

'He ate more of them than the Carpenter,' said Tweedledee. 'He ate faster, you see.'

'Oh!' said Alice. 'Well then, I like the Carpenter best.'

'But he ate as many as he could get,' said Tweedledum.

'Well, they were *both* very unkind—' Alice began, then stopped when she heard a noise in the wood. It sounded like a wild animal. 'What's that?' she asked, afraid.

'It's only the Red King snoring,' said Tweedledee. 'Come and look at him.'

The brothers each took one of Alice's hands and they went through the wood to where the King was sleeping.

'Doesn't he look *lovely*?' said Tweedledum.

Alice really couldn't agree. The King was lying in a very untidy way, and was snoring loudly.

'He's dreaming now,' said Tweedledee, 'and what do you think he's dreaming about?'

'Nobody can guess that,' said Alice.

'Why, about *you!*' Tweedledee said. 'And if he stops dreaming about you, where do you think you will be?'

'Where I am now, of course,' said Alice.

'Oh no!' said Tweedledum. 'You'll be nowhere. You're only a kind of thing in his dream! If he wakes up, you'll go out – bang! – just like a light!'

'What nonsense!' Alice said crossly. 'And if *I'm* only a kind of thing in his dream, what are *you*, I'd like to know.'

'The same!' the brothers cried together.

'Shhh! Don't make so much noise,' Alice said. 'You'll wake him up.'

'He's dreaming now,' said Tweedledee.

21

'How can *you* wake him,' said Tweedledum, 'when you're only one of the things in his dream? You know very well that you're not real.'

'I *am* real!' said Alice, and began to cry.

'I don't know why you're crying,' Tweedledee said unkindly. 'You won't become real that way.'

'I know they're talking nonsense,' Alice thought to herself, 'and there really isn't anything to cry about.' She gave herself a little shake, then said, 'I think I must find my way out of the wood now, because it's getting very dark. Do you think it's going to rain?'

'Possibly,' Tweedledum said, opening a large umbrella.

It was now getting very dark indeed and Alice thought there must be a storm coming. 'What a thick black cloud that is!' she said. 'And how fast it comes! Why, I do believe it's got wings!'

'It's the crow!' Tweedledee shouted fearfully. The two brothers turned to run and had disappeared in a moment.

Alice ran too, and hid under some low trees. 'It can't get me under here,' she thought, 'but I wish its wings didn't make so much wind. It's blowing everything around terribly – and look! Here's somebody's shawl flying through the air!'

5

The White Queen

She caught the shawl as she spoke, and looked around for the owner. A moment later the White Queen came running wildly through the wood. Alice went to meet her with the shawl.

'I'm pleased I was able to catch it for you,' Alice said, as she helped the Queen to put on her shawl again. 'Am I speaking to the White Queen?' she added politely.

'Yes,' said the Queen, as she pulled helplessly at her shawl. 'Oh dear! I don't know what's the matter with my shawl today. I think it's angry with me. I've pinned it here, and I've pinned it there, but it's just not happy.'

'But it can't go straight, you know, if you pin it all on one side,' Alice said, as she gently put it right for her. 'And I'm afraid your hair is terribly untidy.'

Alice pinned up the Queen's hair more tidily.

'The hairbrush is lost in it somewhere,' the Queen said unhappily.

Alice carefully took out the brush and pinned up the Queen's hair more tidily. 'There, you look better now,' she said. 'But really you should have a lady's maid.'

'I'd be happy to take *you*,' the Queen said. 'Twopence a week, and jam every other day.'

'I don't want you to employ *me*,' Alice said, laughing. 'And I don't like jam.'

'It's very good jam,' said the Queen.

'Well, I don't want any *today*, thank you.'

'But you can't have jam today,' the Queen said. 'It's jam tomorrow and jam yesterday – but never jam today.'

'It must be "jam today" *sometimes*,' Alice argued.

'No, it isn't,' said the Queen. 'It's jam every *other* day. Today isn't any *other* day, you know.'

'I don't understand that,' said Alice, very puzzled.

'That's because we live backwards here,' explained the Queen kindly. 'It's always a little difficult at first.'

'Live backwards!' Alice repeated, in great surprise. 'I never heard of anybody doing that.'

'But there's one very useful thing about it,' the Queen went on, 'you can remember things both ways.'

'I only remember things one way,' Alice said. 'I can't remember things before they happen.'

The King's Messenger is in prison now.

24

'That's not very useful,' said the Queen. 'I can remember things that happened the week after next. For example, the King's Messenger is in prison now, but he hasn't done anything wrong yet. His crime will come much later.'

'But what happens if there is no crime,' asked Alice, 'and he doesn't do anything wrong at all? That seems a strange way of—'

At that moment the Queen began to scream very loudly, and to shake her hand around in the air. 'Oh, oh!' she shouted. 'My finger's bleeding! Oh, oh, oh!'

Alice put her hands over her ears. 'What *is* the matter?' she said, in between the Queen's screams. 'Have you cut your finger?'

'I haven't cut it *yet*,' the Queen said, 'but I soon shall – oh, oh, oh!'

'When do you think you will do it?' Alice asked, trying not to laugh.

'When I fasten my shawl again,' the Queen said unhappily, 'one of the pins will come out and – oh, oh!' As she said the words, one of her shawl pins came undone and she quickly took hold of it, trying to fasten it again.

'Take care!' cried Alice. 'You're holding it wrong!' She tried to help the Queen, but it was too late – the pin had already gone deep into the Queen's finger.

'That explains the bleeding, you see,' the Queen said to Alice with a smile. 'Now you understand the way things happen here.'

'But why don't you scream now?' Alice asked, holding her

hands ready to put over her ears again.

'I've done all the screaming already,' said the Queen. 'Why do it all again?'

'It's very difficult to believe,' Alice said, 'that life can happen backwards.'

'Try to believe something a bit easier,' said the Queen helpfully. 'For example, I'm a hundred and one years old.'

'I can't believe *that!*' said Alice.

'Can't you?' the Queen said, shaking her head sadly. 'Try again. Put your hands together and shut your eyes.'

Alice laughed. 'There's no use trying,' she said. 'Nobody can believe *impossible* things.'

'Perhaps you don't work hard enough at it,' said the Queen. 'When I was a child, I worked at it for an hour a day. Why, sometimes I've believed as many as six impossible things before breakfast. There goes my shawl again!'

The pins had come undone again as she spoke, and a sudden wind blew her shawl across a little brook. The Queen went flying after it, and managed to catch it. 'I've got it!' she called happily. 'Now you will see me pin it on again, all by myself.'

'Then I hope your finger is better now?' Alice said very politely, as she crossed the brook after the Queen.

*   *   *   *   *
*   *   *   *
*   *   *   *   *

'Oh, much better!' cried the Queen, her voice getting higher and higher as she went on. 'Much be–etter! Be–e–e–tter!

Be–e–eh!' The last word sounded very like the sound that a sheep makes, and Alice looked at the Queen in surprise.

And indeed, the Queen was now covered in a thick woolly coat, and . . . Alice closed her eyes, then opened them again. She couldn't understand what had happened at all. The wood had disappeared, and she was in a little dark shop – and it really was a *sheep* in front of her, wearing large glasses and sitting calmly on a chair, knitting.

'What do you want to buy?' the Sheep said at last, looking up for a moment from her knitting.

'I'm not sure at the moment,' Alice said gently. 'May I look round first?'

She began to walk round the shop, looking at everything. But every time she looked hard at something, it seemed to move and then appear again a moment later in a different place. So it was difficult to see clearly what was there. She went on walking, and soon realized that the shop was much bigger than she had thought.

'What a strange shop!' Alice said. 'I wish things would keep still!'

A few minutes later the shop became even stranger, because Alice found herself walking beside a large lake, with tall green plants growing round the edge. She put out her hand to pick some, but the plants disappeared when she touched them.

'Oh, what a pity!' said Alice. 'I would like to take some home. They look so pretty.'

'There are lots of other things here,' said the Sheep. 'But you must decide what you want to buy.'

'To buy!' Alice said, jumping a little in surprise. The lake had gone, and she was back in the little dark shop. The Sheep was still knitting, and was looking at her crossly over the top of her glasses.

'I would like to buy an egg, please,' Alice said. 'How much do they cost?'

'Fivepence for one, twopence for two,' the Sheep replied.

'So two are cheaper than one?' Alice said in a surprised voice, taking out her purse.

The Sheep was still knitting.

28

'But you *must* eat them both, if you buy two,' said the Sheep.

'Then I'll have *one*, please,' said Alice, giving the Sheep fivepence.

The Sheep took the money, then said, 'You must get it yourself, you know. It's at the end of the shop.'

The end of the shop was very dark, and was crowded with tables and chairs. Alice could see the egg, but she never seemed to get near it. She almost fell over a chair, and then realized that it was not a chair at all, but a small tree. 'Why are trees growing here?' she wondered. 'This is the strangest shop that I ever saw! And now here's a little brook as well!'

*　　*　　*　　*　　*

*　　*　　*　　*

*　　*　　*　　*　　*

So she went on, wondering more and more at every step. After a while everything had turned into a tree, and she thought that the egg would soon do the same.

6

Humpty Dumpty

But the egg got larger and larger, and more and more like a person. Then Alice saw that it had eyes and a nose and a mouth, and she realized that it was HUMPTY DUMPTY himself.

'It must be him,' she said to herself. 'There he is, sitting on a high wall, and he looks *just* like an egg.'

He was sitting very still and seemed to be asleep, so Alice stood and repeated to herself the words of the song:

> *Humpty Dumpty sat on a wall;*
> *Humpty Dumpty had a great fall.*
> *All the King's horses and all the King's men*
> *Couldn't put Humpty together again.*

'Don't stand there talking to yourself,' said Humpty Dumpty suddenly, opening his eyes. 'Tell me your name.'

'My name is Alice—'

'That's a stupid name!' said Humpty Dumpty. 'What does it mean?'

'*Must* a name mean something?' Alice asked, puzzled.

'Of course it must,' Humpty Dumpty said with a short laugh. '*My* name means the shape I am – and a very good shape it is, too. With a name like yours, you could be almost any shape.'

'Why do you sit out here all alone?' said Alice, not wishing to argue.

'Because there's nobody with me!' cried Humpty Dumpty. 'Did you think I didn't know the answer to *that*? Come, let's have some intelligent conversation now.'

Alice tried to think of something intelligent to say, but couldn't. 'What a beautiful belt you're wearing!' she said, suddenly noticing it.

'That's better,' said Humpty Dumpty, looking pleased. 'Yes, it was a present from the White King and Queen. They

gave it to me for an unbirthday present.'

Alice looked puzzled. 'What is an unbirthday present?'

'A present when it isn't your birthday, of course.'

Alice thought about this. 'I like birthday presents best,' she said at last.

'You don't know what you're talking about!' cried Humpty Dumpty. 'How many days are there in a year?'

'My name is Alice—'

'Three hundred and sixty-five,' said Alice.

'And how many birthdays have you?'

'One.'

'And if you take one from three hundred and sixty-five, what is left?'

31

'Three hundred and sixty-four, of course.'

'So there's only one day when you can get birthday presents,' said Humpty Dumpty, 'but three hundred and sixty-four days when you can get unbirthday presents! There's success for you!'

'I don't know what you mean by "success",' Alice said.

Humpty Dumpty smiled. 'Of course you don't – until I tell you. I meant "there's a clever idea for you!"'

'But "success" doesn't mean "a clever idea",' Alice argued.

'When *I* use a word,' Humpty Dumpty said, looking down his nose at Alice, 'it means just what I choose it to mean – neither more nor less.'

'But *can* you make words have different meanings?' asked Alice.

'Words are difficult things, I agree,' said Humpty Dumpty. 'But you have to be strong with them. Give them orders. Tell them to obey you. They must work hard, and do what they're told!' He banged his hand excitedly on the wall as he spoke.

'You seem very clever with words, Sir,' said Alice politely, hoping to calm him. She was worried about him falling off the wall.

Humpty Dumpty looked pleased. 'I can explain most words, and get them to do what I want,' he said. 'Some of them are like suitcases, you know. They've got several meanings packed up in them. Take poems, for example. One short poem can carry as many meanings as five people's luggage.'

'Somebody repeated a poem to me earlier today,' said Alice. 'It was Tweedledee, I think.'

'Oh, I can repeat any number of poems, if you like,' said Humpty Dumpty.

'Well, not just at the moment,' Alice said quickly, hoping to stop him from beginning.

'This piece was written specially for you,' Humpty Dumpty went on, not listening to her. 'It will amuse you.'

'Thank you,' said Alice sadly. She could not refuse to listen, she thought, if the poem was specially written for her.

> *In winter, when the fields are white,*
> *I sing this song for your delight—*

'But I don't sing it,' he explained.

'Yes, I can see that,' Alice said.

'If you can *see* me singing or not singing, you've better eyes than most people,' said Humpty Dumpty. Alice was silent, and he went on.

> *In spring, when woods are getting green,*
> *I'll try and tell you what I mean.*

'Thank you very much,' said Alice.

> *In summer, when the days are long,*
> *Perhaps you'll understand the song.*
> *In autumn, when the leaves are brown,*
> *Take pen and ink and write it down.*

'I will, if I can remember it so long,' said Alice.

'Don't go on saying things,' Humpty Dumpty said. 'They're not sensible, and I forget where I am.'

> *I sent a message to the fish;*
> *I told them 'This is what I wish.'*
> *The little fishes of the sea,*
> *They sent an answer back to me.*
> *The little fishes' answer was*
> *'We cannot do it, Sir, because—'*

'I'm afraid I don't understand,' said Alice.

'It gets easier as it goes on,' Humpty Dumpty replied.

But the poem went on for a long time, and Alice thought it got harder, not easier, to understand. Then Humpty Dumpty suddenly stopped, and there was a long silence.

'Is that all?' Alice asked politely.

'That's all,' said Humpty Dumpty. 'Goodbye.'

Alice waited a minute, but Humpty Dumpty closed his eyes and did not speak again. So she got up, said 'goodbye', and quietly walked away.

'What an extraordinary person!' she said to herself as she walked. 'I don't think I ever met—' She never finished what she was saying, because at that moment a heavy crash shook the forest from end to end.

7

The Lion and the Unicorn

The next moment soldiers came running through the wood, at first in twos and threes, then ten or twenty together, and at last in great crowds that seemed to fill the forest. Alice got behind a tree and watched them go past.

They were very strange soldiers, she thought. They were always falling over something or other, and when one soldier went down, several more always fell over him. Soon the

They were always falling over something or other.

ground was covered with fallen men.

Then came the horses. With four feet, they managed better than the foot-soldiers, but even they fell more often than not. And when a horse fell, the rider always fell off at once. It was almost like a battle in itself, and Alice decided it would be safer to move on. Soon she came to an open place, where she found the White King sitting on the ground, busily writing in his notebook.

'I've sent them all!' the King cried happily when he saw Alice. 'Did you happen to meet any soldiers, my dear, as you came through the wood?'

'Yes, I did,' said Alice. 'Several thousand, I think.'

'Four thousand two hundred and seven,' the King said, looking at his book. 'I couldn't send all the horses, because two of them are wanted in the game. And I haven't sent the Messengers, Haigha and Hatta. I need them myself, of course – to come and go. One to come, and one to go.'

'I don't think I understand,' said Alice. 'Why one to come and one to go?'

'I've told you,' the King said crossly. 'I must have *two* – to fetch and carry. One to fetch, and one to carry.'

At that moment Haigha, one of the Messengers, arrived. He had very large hands and great eyes, which were always moving wildly from side to side.

'What's the news from town?' said the King.

'I'll whisper it,' said Haigha, putting his mouth close to the King's ear.

Alice was sorry about this, because she wanted to hear the

news too. But, instead of whispering, Haigha shouted at the top of his voice, 'They're at it again!'

'Do you call *that* a whisper?' cried the poor King, jumping up and shaking himself. 'Don't do that again!'

'Who are at it again?' Alice asked.

'The Lion and the Unicorn, of course,' said the King.

'Fighting for the crown?'

'Yes, and it's *my* crown that they're fighting about!' said the King. 'Amusing, isn't it? Let's run and see them.'

They began to run, and as they went, Alice repeated to herself the words of the old song.

> *The Lion and the Unicorn*
> *were fighting for the crown;*
> *The Lion beat the Unicorn*
> *all round the town.*
> *Some gave them white bread*
> *and some gave them brown;*
> *Some gave them plum-cake*
> *and drummed them out of town.*

Soon they saw a great crowd in front of them, and in the middle the Lion and the Unicorn were fighting. Hatta, the other Messenger, was standing at the edge of the crowd, with a cup of tea in one hand and a piece of bread and butter in the other. He looked very unhappy.

'He's only just come out of prison,' Haigha whispered in Alice's ear, 'so he's very hungry and thirsty, you see. How are you, dear child?' he said to Hatta, in a friendly voice.

Hatta looked round, but went on eating his bread and butter and drinking his tea.

'Come, tell us the news!' cried the King. 'How are they getting on with the fight?'

'They're getting on very well,' Hatta said through a mouthful of bread and butter. 'Each of them has been down about eighty-seven times.'

'Then I suppose they'll soon bring the white bread and the brown,' Alice said.

'It's waiting for them now,' said Hatta. 'I'm eating a bit of it myself.'

The fight stopped just then, and the Lion and the Unicorn

*Haigha looked round, but went on
eating his bread and butter and drinking his tea.*

sat down, looking tired.

The King called out, 'Ten minutes for tea!', and Haigha and Hatta began to carry round plates of white and brown bread. Alice took a piece to taste, but it was *very* dry.

'I don't think they'll fight any more today,' the King said to Hatta. 'Go and order the drums to begin.'

As Alice watched him go, she suddenly saw somebody running out of the wood.

'Look!' she cried excitedly. 'There's the White Queen! She came flying out of the wood. How fast those Queens can run!'

'There's probably an enemy after her,' said the King, not looking round. 'That wood's full of them.'

'But aren't you going to help her?' asked Alice, very surprised.

'No use, no use!' said the King. 'She runs so terribly quickly. You can't catch a Queen when she's running.'

At that moment the Unicorn came past, with his hands in his pockets. When he saw Alice, he stopped and looked at her for some minutes. He did not seem to like what he saw.

'What – is – this?' he said at last.

'This is a child!' Haigha said helpfully, coming forward to introduce Alice. 'We only found it today. It's as large as life, and twice as natural!'

'I always thought they were fantastic monsters,' said the Unicorn. 'Is it alive?'

'It can talk,' said Haigha.

The Unicorn looked dreamily at Alice. 'Talk, child.'

Alice smiled. 'I always thought that Unicorns were fantastic

39

monsters, too! I never saw one alive before.'

'Well, we have now met and spoken, so we can believe in each other, yes?' The Unicorn turned to the King. 'Fetch out the plum-cake, old man. I'm tired of brown bread!'

'Certainly, certainly,' said the King, sounding a little frightened. 'Quick, Haigha, open the bag.'

Haigha was carrying a big bag round his neck, and now he took out of it a very large cake, a plate and a knife. He gave them to Alice to hold.

The Lion had joined them while this was going on. He looked very tired and sleepy, and his eyes were half shut. 'What's this?' he said, looking at Alice.

'Ah, what *is* it, then?' the Unicorn cried. 'You'll never guess! *I* couldn't.'

The Lion looked at Alice without interest. 'Are you a vegetable or an animal?' he asked tiredly.

'It's a fantastic monster!' the Unicorn cried, before Alice could reply.

'Then pass round the plum-cake, Monster,' the Lion said, lying down on the ground. 'And you two sit down,' he said to the King and the Unicorn.

The King looked very uncomfortable when he had to sit between the Lion and the Unicorn, but there was no other place for him. His crown nearly fell off because he was shaking so much. The Unicorn looked amused, and then tried to argue with the Lion about who was winning the fight.

'I beat *you* all round the town,' said the Lion angrily. 'And why is the Monster taking so long to cut up the cake?'

'It's very difficult,' said Alice. 'I've cut off several pieces already, but then they join up again immediately!'

'You don't know how to manage looking-glass cakes,' said the Unicorn. 'Pass it round first, and cut it up afterwards.'

This sounded nonsense, but Alice got up and carried the plate round. At once the cake cut itself into three pieces, and then Alice returned to her place with the empty plate.

'Look at my piece of cake!' cried the Unicorn. 'The Monster has given the Lion twice as much as me!'

'She hasn't kept any for herself,' said the Lion. 'Do you like plum-cake, Monster?'

But before Alice could answer, the drums began. The air seemed full of the noise, and it rang and rang through her

'What's this?' the Lion said, looking at Alice.

head. Frightened, Alice began to run and jumped over

*   *   *   *   *

*   *   *   *

*   *   *   *   *

the brook. Then she fell to the ground and put her hands over her ears, trying to shut out the terrible noise.

'If that doesn't drum the Lion and the Unicorn out of town,' she thought to herself, 'nothing ever will!'

Alice fell to the ground and put her hands over her ears.

8

The White Knight

After a while the noise of the drums slowly died away and everything became silent. Alice lifted her head and saw that she was alone, but there, lying at her feet, was the plate on which she had tried to cut the plum-cake.

'So I didn't dream the Lion and the Unicorn, then,' she said to herself. 'But – oh dear! Perhaps we're all part of the same dream. I do hope it's *my* dream, and not the Red King's! I don't like belonging to another person's dream.'

At this moment there was a loud shout, and a Knight in red armour came riding through the forest towards her. Just as he reached her, the horse stopped suddenly.

'You're my prisoner!' the Red Knight cried, as he fell off his horse.

Alice was more worried for the Knight than for herself, but he got up and slowly climbed back on to his horse. He began again to say, 'You're my—', but then another shout rang through the forest. Alice looked round in surprise.

This time it was a White Knight. He rode up to Alice and when his horse stopped, he too fell off at once. He got on again, and then the two Knights sat and looked at each other silently. Alice watched them both, feeling very puzzled.

'She's *my* prisoner, you know!' the Red Knight said at last.

'Yes, but then *I* came and saved her!' the White Knight replied.

'Well, we must fight for her, then,' said the Red Knight, and he began to put on his helmet, which was in the shape of a horse's head.

When the White Knight had got into his helmet as well, the two began fighting each other very noisily. Several times one knocked the other off his horse, but then always fell off himself. Alice got behind a tree, where she could watch more safely.

'What a noise their armour makes when they fall off!' she

Alice got behind a tree,
where she could watch more safely.

said to herself. 'And how calm the horses are! They just stand there like tables while the Knights get on and off!'

The battle ended when they both fell off at the same time. Then they shook hands and the Red Knight got on his horse and rode away. The White Knight came up to Alice.

'I won that battle easily, didn't I?' he said.

'I don't know,' said Alice, uncertainly. 'I don't want to be anybody's prisoner. I want to be a Queen.'

'So you will, when you've crossed the next brook,' said the White Knight. 'I'll see you safe to the end of the wood – and then I must go back, you know. That's the end of my move.'

'Thank you very much,' said Alice. 'May I help you take off your helmet?'

It was difficult to do, but at last the helmet came off.

'Ah, that's better,' said the Knight. He pushed back his long wild hair with both hands, and turned his gentle face and large sad eyes to Alice.

He was a very strange-looking soldier, Alice thought. His armour fitted him very badly, and he had a great many things fastened to himself, and to the horse. There was also a small wooden box on his back, which was upside-down.

'I see you're looking at my little box,' the Knight said in a friendly voice. 'It's my own invention – to keep clothes and sandwiches in. You see I carry it upside-down, and then the rain can't get in.'

'But the things can get *out*,' Alice said gently. 'Did you know that the top was open?'

'No, I didn't,' the Knight said. 'If all the things have fallen out,' he went on unhappily, 'there's no use keeping the box.' He unfastened it as he spoke, and put it carefully on the branch of a tree. 'Perhaps some birds will make a home in it. Now, if you're ready . . . What's that plate for?'

'It was used for plum-cake,' said Alice.

'I think we should take it with us,' the Knight said. 'It'll be useful if we find any plum-cake. Help me to get it into this bag.'

This took a long time to do because the bag was not really big enough and already had a lot of carrots in it. But at last it was done, and they started walking through the forest. It was a slow journey because the Knight was not a good rider. Every time the horse stopped (which it did very often), he fell off in front. When the horse went on again, he fell off behind. Sometimes he fell off sideways as well, and Alice learnt not to walk too close to the horse.

'Perhaps you should have a wooden horse, on wheels,' Alice said with a little laugh, as she helped him get back

Every time the horse stopped, the knight fell off in front.

on his horse for the seventh time.

'Do you think so?' the Knight said seriously. 'Yes, I'll get one. One or two – several.'

As they went, the Knight told her about his many inventions. Alice listened with great interest, but found most of them hard to understand. She was thinking about his invention for turning fish eyes into buttons when she saw, to her surprise, that they had reached the end of the forest.

'You are sad,' the Knight said in a worried voice. 'Let me sing you a song to cheer you up.'

'Is it very long?' Alice asked. She felt that she had heard a great many poems and songs that day.

'It's long,' said the Knight, 'but it's very, *very* beautiful. Everybody that hears me sing it – either they cry, or—' He stopped suddenly.

'Or what?' said Alice.

'Or they don't, you know. The song is called *I'll tell you everything I can*. It's about an old, old man that I met one summer evening long ago, while sitting on the grass.'

Years afterwards Alice could still remember very clearly those strange moments – the Knight's gentle smile as he sang, the sunlight shining on his armour, the horse quietly moving around, and the black shadows of the forest behind.

She stood and listened very carefully, but she did not cry. It was a sad song, certainly, and as the Knight came towards the end, he seemed lost in his own sad dreams.

> *And now, if accidentally I put*
> *My fingers into glue,*

Or try to push a right-hand foot
Into a left-hand shoe,
Or if I drop upon my toe
A very heavy glass,
I cry, as it reminds me so
Of that old man I used to know—
Whose face was kind, whose voice was slow,
Whose hair was whiter than the snow,
Who shook his body to and fro,
And whispered words both sad and low—
That summer evening long ago,
While sitting on the grass.

As the Knight sang the last words, he began to turn his horse round to go back into the forest.

'You've only a little way to go,' he said, 'down the hill and over the brook, and then you'll be a Queen.'

'Thank you very much for coming so far,' said Alice, 'and for the song – I liked it very much.'

'I hope so,' the Knight said worriedly, 'but you didn't cry very much.'

They shook hands, and then the Knight rode slowly away into the forest. Alice stood and watched him for a while.

'It won't be long before he falls off again,' she said to herself. 'Yes – there he goes! Right on his head as usual! But he doesn't seem to mind a bit.'

When he had gone, Alice turned and ran down the hill. 'Now for the last brook, and to be a Queen! How grand it sounds!' A few steps brought her to the edge of the brook.

'What is this on my head?'
Alice said.

'The Eighth Square at last!' she cried, as she jumped over

* * * * *

* * * *

* * * * *

and sat down to rest on the soft green grass. At once she felt something very heavy on her head. 'What *is* this on my head?' she said. 'And how did it get there?' She lifted it off, to see what it was.

It was a golden crown.

9

Queen Alice

'Well, this *is* grand!' said Alice. She got up and walked around for a while, but the crown felt very heavy and strange, so she sat down again. Then she noticed that the Red Queen and the White Queen were now sitting on either side of her. How they had got there, she had no idea. But she was not at all surprised. Nothing could surprise her now in the looking-glass world.

'Now I am a Queen,' said Alice, 'does this mean that the game of chess has finished, or—'

'Speak when you're spoken to!' the Red Queen said. 'Think before you speak, and write it down afterwards.'

'But I only—' Alice began.

'And you can't be a Queen,' the Red Queen went on, 'until you've done your lessons.'

'Are you good at sums?' the White Queen asked. 'What's one and one and one and one and one and one and one?'

'I don't know,' said Alice. 'I lost count. But why—'

'She can't do sums,' said the Red Queen. 'What about languages? And can you read?'

'Of course I can read!' Alice said. 'And I know a little French, but I really don't see why—'

'It's clear,' said the White Queen, shaking her head sadly, 'that she wants to argue about *something*, but she doesn't know what to argue about!'

Alice decided it would be safer to say nothing, and for a while there was silence. Then the Red Queen said to the White Queen, 'I invite you to Alice's party this afternoon.'

'And I invite *you*,' the White Queen replied. 'But I must have a rest first,' she went on. 'I am *so* sleepy.'

'And so must I,' said the Red Queen. She looked at Alice. 'You can sing to us, to help us sleep.'

Then the two Queens put their heads against Alice's shoulders. In a moment they were both asleep, and snoring loudly.

After a while the snoring seemed to change and began to

In a moment the two Queens were both asleep, and snoring loudly.

sound almost like music. Alice thought that she could even hear some words. She listened hard, and suddenly she found that the Queens had disappeared, and she was standing in front of a tall and very grand-looking doorway. Above the door were the words QUEEN ALICE in large letters.

Alice knocked, and the door flew open. There seemed to be hundreds of voices singing, and Alice could now hear the words very clearly. They went like this:

> *Then fill up the glasses with everything nice,*
> *And cover the table with buttons and rice.*
> *Put cats in the coffee, and salt in the tea—*
> *And welcome Queen Alice with thirty-times-three!*

'I suppose I should go in,' Alice said to herself. So in she went, and at once everyone in the hall became silent.

As she walked down the long hall, she saw that there were animals, birds, and even a few flowers among the crowd seated round the table. At the top there were three chairs; the Red and White Queens had taken two of them, but the middle one was empty. Alice sat down, feeling a little uncomfortable and wishing that someone would speak.

At last the Red Queen began. 'You've missed the fish. Bring the meat now!' And at once the waiters put a large joint of meat in front of Alice.

The joint of meat stood up and curtsied to Alice.

But before she could begin to cut up the joint, the Red Queen spoke again. 'Let me introduce you to the joint,' she said. 'Alice – Meat. Meat – Alice.'

The joint of meat then stood up on the plate and curtsied to Alice. Alice, feeling both frightened and amused, picked up the knife and fork. 'May I give you some meat?' she said, looking from one Queen to the other.

'Certainly not!' the Red Queen said. 'It isn't

polite to cut anyone you've been introduced to. Take away the joint!'

The waiters immediately carried away the joint, and brought a large plum-pudding in its place.

'Please don't introduce me to the pudding,' said Alice quickly, 'or we shall get no dinner at all.'

But the Red Queen said loudly, 'Pudding – Alice. Alice – Pudding. Take away the pudding!' And the waiters took it away at once.

Then Alice decided to give an order herself. 'Waiter! Bring back the pudding!' When the pudding appeared again, she quickly cut off a piece and gave it to the Red Queen.

'That's *really* friendly!' said the Pudding. 'How would *you* like someone to cut a piece out of *you*?'

Alice was too surprised to speak.

'Say something,' said the Red Queen. 'You can't leave all the conversation to the pudding!'

By this time the party was beginning to get very noisy, and more and more strange things were happening. Bottles and plates were now walking around on the table, arm in arm, and the White Queen began to whisper in Alice's ear a long poem about fishes. Then the Red Queen screamed at the top of her voice, 'Let's drink to Queen Alice's health!'

Some of the animals put their glasses upside-down on their heads, others got inside them or knocked them over on the table. The forks began to dance with the spoons, and the noise got wilder and wilder. The White Queen said in Alice's ear, 'You must stand up and give thanks now, you know.'

Alice stood up. 'I must stop all this!' she cried, and she took hold of the table-cloth with both hands. One good pull, and everything came crashing down on the floor.

'And now for *you*!' she went on, turning to the Red Queen, who had suddenly become very much smaller and was running around on

One good pull,
and everything came crashing down on the floor.

the table. '*You* started all this trouble, and I'll shake you into a kitten! Yes, I will!'

10
Shaking

She took the Red Queen off the table as she spoke, and shook her backwards and forwards, very hard.

The Red Queen did not try to fight or escape . . . but her face grew very small, and her eyes got large and green . . . and, as Alice went on shaking her, she grew shorter – and fatter – and softer – and rounder – and . . .

11
Waking

. . . and it really *was* a kitten, after all.

12
Who dreamed it?

'You shouldn't be so noisy, Your Majesty,' Alice said to the black kitten. 'You've woken me out of a very nice dream. I've been all through the looking-glass world. And I think that *you* were the Red Queen, weren't you?'

It is impossible to guess if a kitten is saying 'yes' or 'no'. Alice looked among the chessmen on the table until she found the Red Queen. Then she sat on the carpet and put the kitten and the Queen to look at each other.

'Curtsy while you're thinking what to say,' Alice said, with a little laugh. 'It saves time, remember!'

But the kitten turned its head away and wouldn't look at the Queen.

'Now, Kitty,' Alice went on, 'who was it who dreamed it all, do you think? No, listen – don't start washing your paws now. You see, Kitty, it was either me or the Red King. He was part of my dream, of course – but then I was part of his dream too! *Was* it the Red King, Kitty?'

But the kitten began to wash its other paw, and pretended it hadn't heard the question.

Who do *you* think was dreaming?

GLOSSARY

beetle a kind of insect, with hard, shiny wings
believe to think that something is real or true
brook a very small, narrow river
certain sure
crow a large black bird
curtsy to bend your knees politely to someone, e.g. a queen
hedge a line of small trees and bushes growing close together
insect a very small kind of animal with six legs, e.g. a fly
invention something new that you have made yourself
jam a sweet food, made by cooking fruit and sugar
kitten a baby cat
maid a woman or girl who works in another person's house
Majesty you say 'Your Majesty' when speaking to a queen or king
messenger somebody who carries messages
monster a very strange, sometimes frightening, person or animal
nonsense silly or stupid talk or ideas
paw the foot of a cat or kitten
poem a piece of writing in verse
pudding sweet food that you eat at the end of a meal
puzzled not understanding something
snore to make a loud noise while you are asleep
sums adding numbers together, e.g. 2 and 2 is 4
unicorn an imaginary animal, like a horse with a horn on its head

JABBERWOCKY

The words in the poem on page 5 were invented by Lewis Carroll, and are not real English words. So they can mean what you choose them to mean.

Through the Looking-Glass

ACTIVITIES

Before Reading

1 **Read the story introduction on the first page of the book, and the back cover. What do you know now about this story? Circle the right words to complete this passage.**

In the looking-glass world Alice is first a *knight / pawn* and later becomes a *queen / king* in the *Fourth / Eighth* Square. She travels by *train / bus* through the Third Square, finds a *lake / mountain* in the Fifth Square, and goes through a *valley / wood* in the Seventh Square.

  It is a very strange game of *cards / chess*. The pieces *talk / are silent* all the time. Time runs *forwards / backwards* and the *White / Red* Queen can remember things from the *future / past*.

2 **How will the dream end? Can you guess? Choose one of these ideas.**

1 Alice climbs back through the looking-glass and wakes up.
2 The Red King wakes up and Alice disappears, because the Red King was real and Alice was part of *his* dream.
3 In the dream Alice shakes the Red Queen, who turns into a black kitten, and Alice wakes up.
4 Alice's sister comes into the room, finds Alice asleep in an armchair, and wakes her up.
5 In the dream Alice falls into a lake of very cold water, which wakes her up.

60

While Reading

Read Chapters 1 and 2. Choose the best question-word for these questions, and then answer them.

What / Which / Why

1 . . . kitten began it all?
2 . . . happened to the looking-glass above the fireplace?
3 . . . chessmen did Alice pick up and put on the table?
4 . . . couldn't Alice read the poem *Jabberwocky* at first?
5 . . . flower spoke to Alice first?
6 . . . can't flowers talk in most gardens?
7 . . . did Alice see from the top of the hill?
8 . . . was Alice surprised when she and the Red Queen stopped running?

Read Chapters 3 and 4, and complete these sentences with words from the story.

1 Alice jumped over a _____ to get into the _____ square.
2 On the _____ the Inspector asked for Alice's _____.
3 The small voice in Alice's ear was the voice of an _____.
4 In the wood Alice could not _____ her own name.
5 Alice had to listen to a long _____ from Tweedledee.
6 Alice felt _____ for the Oysters because the Walrus and the Carpenter _____ them.
7 The Red King was lying asleep in the wood and _____ loudly.

Before you read Chapter 5 (*The White Queen*), can you guess what happens next? Choose some of these ideas.

The White Queen . . .

1 repeats a long poem to Alice.
2 explains about living backwards.
3 gives Alice a present.

4 offers Alice a job.
5 turns into a crow.
6 turns into a sheep.

Read Chapters 5 and 6. Are these sentences true (T) or false (F)? Rewrite the false ones with the right information.

1 The White Queen's maid would have jam every day.
2 The White Queen screamed after she cut her finger.
3 In the shop Alice decided to do some knitting.
4 Buying one egg was more expensive than buying two eggs.
5 Humpty Dumpty's name did not mean anything.
6 You can get an unbirthday present on one day in a year.
7 Humpty Dumpty thought that words were like suitcases, and could carry a lot of meanings.
8 The crash at the end was Humpty Dumpty's great fall.

Read Chapters 7 and 8. Who said this, and to whom? What, or who, were they talking about?

1 'I must have *two* – to fetch and carry. One to fetch, and one to carry.'
2 'They're at it again!'
3 'It's waiting for them now. I'm eating a bit of it myself.'
4 'There's probably an enemy after her. That wood's full of them.'

5 'It's as large as life, and twice as natural!'

6 'The Monster has given the Lion twice as much as me!'

7 'Well, we must fight for her, then.'

8 'It's my own invention – to keep clothes and sandwiches in.'

9 'It's long, but it's very, *very* beautiful.'

10 'Yes – there he goes! Right on his head as usual!'

Before you read the end of the story, can you guess what happens now that Alice is a Queen? Choose Y (yes) or N (no) for each sentence.

1 Alice loses her crown and becomes a pawn again. Y/N

2 The Red Queen tells Alice to think before she speaks. Y/N

3 Alice takes the Red Knight prisoner. Y/N

4 Alice suddenly moves back to the fourth square. Y/N

5 There is a dinner party for Queen Alice. Y/N

6 Alice meets the White Bishop at the dinner party. Y/N

7 Alice is introduced to a plum-pudding at the party. Y/N

8 Alice has to begin a new game of chess. Y/N

9 The party is wild and noisy, and Alice tries to stop it. Y/N

10 Something very strange happens to the Red Queen. Y/N

11 The White Knight appears at the party, and takes Alice away on his horse. Y/N

12 The Red King dies, and the game of chess is finished. Y/N

Read Chapters 9 to 12. How did Alice's dream finish in the end? How many of your guesses were right?

After Reading

1 Complete the sentences with the names of characters from the story (one name is needed twice). Each sentence has another, shorter gap. Choose one word to fill this gap.

Tweedledum and Tweedledee / the Lion and the Unicorn / Haigha and Hatta / Humpty Dumpty / the Red Queen / the Red King / the White Queen / the White King / the Red Knight / the White Knight

1 _____ were _____'s messengers. He had to have two of them – one to come, and one to _____.

2 _____ told Alice all about his many _____; one of them was a box which he carried upside-down on his back.

3 'When *I* use a _____,' said _____ to Alice, 'it means just what I choose it to mean – neither more nor less.'

4 _____ told Alice she could believe six _____ things before breakfast, but it was easier if you shut your eyes.

5 _____ were brothers. They told Alice that she wasn't _____, and was just part of _____'s dream.

6 _____ took Alice prisoner, but then he had to fight a _____ with _____, which he lost, so he rode away.

7 At the party _____ told Alice that it wasn't polite to cut and eat someone you had been _____ to.

8 _____ had never seen a child before, so they thought that Alice was a fantastic _____.

2 **Alice wrote a poem about her dream, but the lines are in the wrong order. Put them in the right order for the story. Start at number 3 and think about the *sound* at the end of the line.**

1 Then there was the White Knight, riding through the trees,
2 I pulled off a table-cloth – but the dream ended there.
3 I once played a kind of chess you never learn in books,
4 I also met the White King, and in a crowded town
5 Meeting Humpty Dumpty, and waiting for his fall.
6 And when I had a Queen's crown in the Eighth Square,
7 Running with the Red Queen, and jumping over brooks,
8 A lion and a unicorn were fighting for his crown.
9 Singing me his sad song, hoping it would please.
10 Talking with the White Queen, and pinning on her shawl,

3 **Here is a poem like Humpty Dumpty's for you to finish. In the middle of the lines, circle the best word. For each gap, choose one word from the list. (Two words have the right meaning. Which are they, and why is one of them better?)**

evening, gold, grow, night, open, red, sleep, snore

In spring, when *(mountains/trees/roads)* lose their snow,
I like to watch the flowers _____.
In summer, when the *(moon/sun/star)* is bright,
I walk through fields and woods till _____.
In autumn, when the *(rivers/leaves/hills)* turn _____,
I know the *(week/month/year)* is growing old.
In winter, when the *(rain/snow/fog)* is deep,
I sit beside the *(television/window/fire)* and _____.

4 Find the **twenty-six** words hidden in this word search, and draw lines through them. Words go from left to right, and from top to bottom. They are all four letters or more.

I	K	N	I	G	H	T	T	S	C	A	K	E	J
A	F	M	T	O	M	P	O	M	H	I	L	L	R
P	A	W	N	R	O	U	F	O	R	E	S	T	W
I	N	S	E	C	T	D	A	N	N	S	D	J	K
A	T	M	H	Y	D	D	E	S	C	Q	B	B	I
S	A	S	O	T	R	I	E	T	R	U	R	E	T
H	S	R	R	D	E	N	A	E	O	A	O	L	T
E	T	Y	S	B	A	G	U	R	W	R	O	I	E
E	I	T	E	N	M	E	V	Q	N	E	K	E	N
P	C	E	R	J	P	A	M	U	T	O	D	V	L
M	O	V	E	N	O	N	S	E	N	S	E	E	I
P	U	Z	Z	L	E	D	A	E	K	I	N	G	O
H	E	D	G	E	M	Y	U	N	I	C	O	R	N

5 Here is Alice, writing about her dream in her diary. Complete it with some of the words from the word search.

So many _____ things happened in looking-glass world! The White _____ turned into a _____, and the Red _____ turned into a _____. The White _____ nearly lost his _____ to a _____ and a _____, and the Red _____ was always snoring. The person I liked best was the White _____. He was so gentle, so sad. He took me through the _____ in the seventh _____, and was always falling off his _____.

But it was all _____, of course. You can't _____ any of it.

6 **Look at the word search again, and write down all the letters that don't have a line through them. (Begin with the first line, and go across each line to the end.) You should have forty-five letters, which will make a sentence of ten words.**

1 What is the sentence, and who said it to Alice?
2 What was the speaker offering Alice at the time?
3 What do you do with the thing in the sentence?
4 When would Alice get this thing?

7 **In looking-glass world you have to do some very strange things. Match these halves of sentences to explain.**

1 If you want to meet people in a garden, . . .
2 If you want to stay in the same place, . . .
3 If you want to get somewhere different, . . .
4 If you travel by train, . . .
5 If you want to give people pieces of cake, . . .
6 And curtsy while you're thinking what to say . . .
7 you must run twice as fast.
8 you should pass it round first and cut it up afterwards.
9 you must walk away from them.
10 because it saves time.
11 you should buy a return ticket at every station.
12 you have to run very fast.

8 **What did you think about the story of Alice's dream?**

1 Which parts of the story did you enjoy most? Why?
2 Which was your favourite character? Why?

ABOUT THE AUTHOR

Lewis Carroll (his real name was Charles Lutwidge Dodgson) was born in 1832, and was the third child of a family of eleven children. As a child, Charles was very good at writing word games and puzzles, and later he was also good at Latin and mathematics. He went to Rugby School, and then to Christ Church at the University of Oxford. He taught mathematics at Christ Church from 1855 until his death in 1898.

Dodgson wrote books about mathematics, and he was also a very good photographer, but his most famous works are the two *Alice* stories. *Alice's Adventures in Wonderland* began as a story told to a real little girl, called Alice Liddell, during a boat trip on the river one summer, and was published as a book in 1865. The second story about Alice, called *Through the Looking-Glass and What Alice Found There*, followed in 1871, and in 1876 came Dodgson's third famous nonsense book, *The Hunting of the Snark*. The two *Alice* stories, full of clever word games and verses, are among the most famous children's books ever written. They are also important because they were the first stories for children which did not try to teach them to be good.

Through the Looking-Glass is enjoyed by both adults and children, and the ideas and characters from the story are now part of our language. We talk about giving and receiving 'unbirthday presents'; we have conversations about 'shoes and ships and sealing wax, cabbages and kings'. And when we hear a promise that we don't believe, we know it's 'jam tomorrow and jam yesterday, but never jam today'.

ABOUT BOOKWORMS

OXFORD BOOKWORMS LIBRARY
*Classics • True Stories • Fantasy & Horror • Human Interest
Crime & Mystery • Thriller & Adventure*

The OXFORD BOOKWORMS LIBRARY offers a wide range of original and adapted stories, both classic and modern, which take learners from elementary to advanced level through six carefully graded language stages:

Stage 1 (400 headwords)	**Stage 4** (1400 headwords)
Stage 2 (700 headwords)	**Stage 5** (1800 headwords)
Stage 3 (1000 headwords)	**Stage 6** (2500 headwords)

More than fifty titles are also available on cassette, and there are many titles at Stages 1 to 4 which are specially recommended for younger learners. In addition to the introductions and activities in each Bookworm, resource material includes photocopiable test worksheets and Teacher's Handbooks, which contain advice on running a class library and using cassettes, and the answers for the activities in the books.

Several other series are linked to the OXFORD BOOKWORMS LIBRARY. They range from highly illustrated readers for young learners, to playscripts, non-fiction readers, and unsimplified texts for advanced learners.

Oxford Bookworms Starters *Oxford Bookworms Factfiles*
Oxford Bookworms Playscripts *Oxford Bookworms Collection*

Details of these series and a full list of all titles in the OXFORD BOOKWORMS LIBRARY can be found in the *Oxford English* catalogues. A selection of titles from the OXFORD BOOKWORMS LIBRARY can be found on the next pages.

Alice's Adventures in Wonderland

LEWIS CARROLL

Retold by Jennifer Bassett

There, on top of the mushroom, was a large caterpillar, smoking a pipe. After a while the Caterpillar took the pipe out of its mouth and said to Alice in a slow, sleepy voice, 'Who are *you*?'

What strange things happen when Alice falls down the rabbit-hole and into Wonderland! She has conversations with the Caterpillar and the Cheshire Cat, goes to the Mad Hatter's tea party, plays croquet with the King and Queen of Hearts . . .

The Railway Children

EDITH NESBIT

Retold by John Escott

'We have to leave our house in London,' Mother said to the children. 'We're going to live in the country, in a little house near a railway line.'

And so begins a new life for Roberta, Peter, and Phyllis. They become the railway children – they know all the trains, Perks the station porter is their best friend, and they have many adventures on the railway line.

But why has their father had to go away? Where is he, and will he ever come back?

The Secret Garden

FRANCES HODGSON BURNETT

Retold by Clare West

Little Mary Lennox is a bad-tempered, disagreeable child. When her parents die in India, she is sent back to England to live with her uncle in a big, lonely, old house.

There is nothing to do all day except walk in the gardens – and watch the robin flying over the high walls of the secret garden . . . which has been locked for ten years. And no one has the key.

Moondial

HELEN CRESSWELL

Retold by John Escott

'Moondial!' As Minty spoke the word, a cold wind went past her, and her ears were filled with a thousand frightened voices. She shut her eyes and put her hands over her ears – and the voices and the wind went away. Minty opened her eyes . . . *and knew that she was in a different morning, not the one she had woken up to.*

And so Minty's strange adventure begins – a journey through time into the past, where she finds Tom, and Sarah . . . and the evil Miss Vole.

The Wind in the Willows

KENNETH GRAHAME

Retold by Jennifer Bassett

Down by the river bank, where the wind whispers through the willow trees, is a very pleasant place to have a lunch party with a few friends. But life is not always so peaceful for the Mole and the Water Rat. There is the time, for example, when Toad gets interested in motor-cars – goes mad about them in fact . . .

The story of the adventures of Mole, Rat, Badger, and Toad has been loved by young and old for almost a hundred years.

The Whispering Knights

PENELOPE LIVELY

Retold by Clare West

'I don't know that you have done anything wrong,' Miss Hepplewhite said. 'But it is possible that you have done something rather dangerous.'

William and Susie thought they were just playing a game when they cooked a witch's brew in the old barn and said a spell over it, but Martha was not so sure. And indeed, the three friends soon learn that they have called up something dark and evil out of the distant past . . .